Compiled by
the Daughters of St. Paul

Illustrated by
Mary Joseph Peterson, FSP

Illustrator Assistant
Laura Rosemarie McGowan, FSP

Pauline
BOOKS & MEDIA
Boston

INTRODUCTORY RITES

Stand

PRIEST: In the name of the Father, and of the Son, and of the Holy Spirit.

PEOPLE: **Amen.**

PRIEST: …to prepare ourselves to celebrate the sacred mysteries, let us call to mind our sins.

PEOPLE:

I confess to almighty God, and to you, my brothers and sisters, that I have sinned through my own fault *(We tap our chest with our right hand.)*

in my thoughts and in my words, in what I have done, and in what I have failed to do; and I ask blessed Mary, ever virgin, all the angels and saints, and you, my brothers and sisters, to pray for me to the Lord our God.

(Sometimes we use a different prayer.)

PRIEST: May almighty God have mercy on us, forgive us our sins, and bring us to everlasting life.

PEOPLE: **Amen.**

PRIEST: Lord, have mercy.

PEOPLE: **Lord, have mercy.**

PRIEST: Christ, have mercy.

PEOPLE: **Christ, have mercy.**

PRIEST: Lord, have mercy.

PEOPLE: **Lord, have mercy.**

PRIEST AND PEOPLE:

Glory to God in the highest, and peace to his people on earth.

Lord God, heavenly King,
almighty God and Father,
    we worship you, we give you thanks,
    we praise you for your glory.
Lord Jesus Christ, only Son of the
    Father,
Lord God, Lamb of God,
you take away the sin of the world:
    have mercy on us;
you are seated at the right hand of the
    Father:
    receive our prayer.

For you alone are the Holy One,
you alone are the Lord,
you alone are the Most High,
    Jesus Christ,
    with the Holy Spirit,
    in the glory of God the Father.

Amen.

The priest prays for all our needs.

People: **Amen.**

The Word of God

LITURGY OF THE WORD

Sit

We listen to the Word of God.

At the end of each reading the reader says: The word of the Lord.

PEOPLE: **Thanks be to God.**

Stand

PRIEST OR DEACON: The Lord be with you.

PEOPLE: **And also with you.**

PRIEST OR DEACON: A reading from the holy gospel according to _____ *(the name of the Gospel writer):*

PEOPLE: **Glory to you, Lord.**

At the end of the Gospel reading, the priest or deacon says:
The gospel of the Lord.

PEOPLE: **Praise to you, Lord Jesus Christ.**

Sit

The priest or deacon explains the readings from God's Word to us.

Stand

We tell God that we believe everything he has taught us.

<small>PRIEST AND PEOPLE:</small>

We believe in one God,
    the Father, the Almighty,
    maker of heaven and earth,
    of all that is seen and unseen.

We believe in one Lord, Jesus Christ,
    the only Son of God,
    eternally begotten of the Father,
    God from God, Light from Light,
    true God from true God,
    begotten, not made, one in Being
      with the Father.
    Through him all things were made.
    For us men and for our salvation
      he came down from heaven:

(Here we bow until after the words "and became man.")

by the power of the Holy Spirit
he was born of the Virgin Mary,
and became man.

For our sake he was crucified under
Pontius Pilate;
he suffered, died, and was buried.
On the third day he rose again
in fulfillment of the Scriptures;
he ascended into heaven
and is seated at the right hand of
the Father.

He will come again in glory to judge
the living and the dead,
and his kingdom will have no end.

We believe in the Holy Spirit, the
Lord, the giver of life,
who proceeds from the Father and
the Son.
With the Father and the Son he is
worshiped and glorified.

He has spoken through the
    Prophets.
We believe in one holy catholic and
    apostolic Church.
We acknowledge one baptism for
    the forgiveness of sins.
We look for the resurrection of the
    dead,
    and the life of the world to come.
    Amen.

*The Apostles' Creed is prayed in Canada
and in some Masses for children:*

PRIEST AND PEOPLE:
I believe in God, the Father almighty,
    creator of heaven and earth.

I believe in Jesus Christ, his only Son,
    our Lord.
    He was conceived by the power of
        the Holy Spirit
        and born of the Virgin Mary.
    He suffered under Pontius Pilate,
        was crucified, died, and was buried.

He descended to the dead.
On the third day he rose again.
He ascended into heaven,
   and is seated at the right hand of
    the Father.
He will come again to judge the
   living and the dead.

I believe in the Holy Spirit,
   the holy catholic Church,
   the communion of saints,
   the forgiveness of sins,
   the resurrection of the body,
   and the life everlasting. Amen.

Next we pray for all the people in the world.
   Lord, hear our prayer.

LITURGY OF THE EUCHARIST

PRESENTATION OF THE GIFTS

Sit

Now some people carry bread and wine to the priest. The bread and wine will become the Body and Blood of Jesus.

We offer God gifts of bread and wine.

PREPARATION OF THE GIFTS

PRIEST: Blessed are you, Lord, God of all creation. Through your goodness we have this bread to offer, which earth has given and human hands have made. It will become for us the bread of life.

PEOPLE: **Blessed be God for ever.**

PRIEST: Blessed are you, Lord, God of all creation. Through your goodness we have this wine to offer, fruit of the vine and work of human hands. It will become our spiritual drink.

PEOPLE: **Blessed be God for ever.**

PRIEST: Pray, brethren, that our sacrifice may be acceptable to God, the almighty Father.

Stand

PEOPLE: **May the Lord accept the sacrifice at your hands for the praise and glory of his name, for our good and the good of all his Church.**

PRIEST: The Lord be with you.

PEOPLE: **And also with you.**

PRIEST: Lift up your hearts.

PEOPLE: **We lift them up to the Lord.**

PRIEST: Let us give thanks to the Lord our God.

PEOPLE: **It is right to give him thanks and praise.**

The priest begins the most important prayer of the Mass. It is called the Eucharistic Prayer. At the end of the first part of this prayer, we sing or pray with the priest:

PRIEST AND PEOPLE:
**Holy, holy, holy Lord, God of power
    and might,
heaven and earth are full of your glory.
    Hosanna in the highest.**

**Blessed is he who comes in the name
    of the Lord.
    Hosanna in the highest.**

Kneel

EUCHARISTIC PRAYER III

The priest prays this prayer or one like it:

Father, you are holy indeed,
and all creation rightly gives you praise.
All life, all holiness comes from you
through your Son,
    Jesus Christ our Lord,
by the working of the Holy Spirit.
From age to age you gather a people to
    yourself,
so that from east to west
a perfect offering may be made
to the glory of your name.

And so, Father, we bring you these gifts.
We ask you to make them holy by the
    power of your Spirit,
that they may become the body and
    blood
of your Son, our Lord Jesus Christ,
at whose command we celebrate this
    eucharist.

On the night he was betrayed,
he took bread and gave you thanks and
   praise.
He broke the bread, gave it to his
   disciples, and said:

**Take this, all of you, and eat it:
this is my body which will be given up
for you.**

*The bread becomes the Body of Christ.
It still looks like bread. It still tastes like
bread. But it really is the Body of Christ!*

PRIEST: When supper was ended, he
took the cup.

Again he gave you thanks and praise,
gave the cup to his disciples, and said:

**Take this, all of you, and drink from it:
this is the cup of my blood,
the blood of the new and everlasting
covenant.**

19

**It will be shed for you and for all
so that sins may be forgiven.
Do this in memory of me.**

*The wine becomes the Blood of Christ.
It still looks like wine. It still tastes like
wine. But it really is the Blood of Christ!
We adore Jesus Christ, present under the
appearance of bread and wine.*

PRIEST: Let us proclaim the mystery of
faith:

PRIEST AND PEOPLE:
**Christ has died,
Christ is risen,
Christ will come again.**

(Sometimes we use a different prayer.)

PRIEST: Father, calling to mind the death
your Son endured for our salvation, his
glorious resurrection and ascension into
heaven, and ready to greet him when he
comes again, we offer you in thanksgiving this holy and living sacrifice.

Look with favor on your Church's
    offering,
and see the Victim whose death has
reconciled us to yourself.
Grant that we, who are nourished by
    his body and blood,
may be filled with his Holy Spirit,
and become one body, one spirit in Christ.

May he make us an everlasting gift
    to you
and enable us to share in the inheritance
    of your saints,
with Mary, the virgin Mother of God;
with the apostles, the martyrs,
(Saint _____) and all your saints,
on whose constant intercession we rely
    for help.

Lord, may this sacrifice,
which has made our peace with you,
advance the peace and salvation of all
    the world.

Strengthen in faith and love your
    pilgrim Church on earth;
your servant, Pope _____,
    our bishop _____,

and all the bishops, with the clergy and
the entire people your Son has
gained for you.

Father, hear the prayers of the family
you have gathered here before
you. In mercy and love unite all
your children wherever they
may be.
Welcome into your kingdom our
departed brothers and sisters, and all
who have left this world in your
friendship.
We hope to enjoy for ever the vision of
your glory,
through Christ our Lord, from whom
all good things come.

Through him,
with him,
in him,
in the unity of the Holy Spirit,
all glory and honor is yours,

almighty Father,
for ever and ever.

PEOPLE: **Amen.**

COMMUNION RITE

Stand

PRIEST: Let us pray with confidence to the Father in the words our Savior gave us.

PRIEST AND PEOPLE:
**Our Father, who art in heaven,
hallowed be thy name;
thy kingdom come;
thy will be done on earth
    as it is in heaven.
Give us this day our daily bread;
and forgive us our trespasses
as we forgive those who trespass
    against us;
and lead us not into temptation,
but deliver us from evil.**

PRIEST: Deliver us, Lord, from every
    evil,
and grant us peace in our day.
In your mercy keep us free from sin
and protect us from all anxiety
as we wait in joyful hope
for the coming of our Savior,
    Jesus Christ.

PEOPLE: **For the kingdom, the power
and the glory are yours, now and for
ever.**

THE SIGN OF PEACE

PRIEST: Lord Jesus Christ, you said to
    your apostles:
I leave you peace, my peace I give
    you.
Look not on our sins, but on the
    faith of your Church,
and grant us the peace and unity of
    your kingdom
where you live for ever and ever.

PEOPLE: **Amen.**

PRIEST: The peace of the Lord be with you always.

PEOPLE: **And also with you.**

PRIEST OR DEACON: Let us offer each other the sign of peace.

We wish the peace of Jesus to each other by shaking hands with the people near us.

Breaking of the Bread

The priest breaks the bread into smaller pieces, just as Jesus did at the Last Supper. Even though we all receive separate pieces in Holy Communion, we all receive the one Jesus.

People: **Lamb of God, you take away the sins of the world:**

have mercy on us.

Lamb of God, you take away the sins of the world:

have mercy on us.

Lamb of God, you take away the sins of the world:

grant us peace.

Holy Communion

Kneel

Priest: This is the Lamb of God who takes away the sins of the world. Happy are those who are called to his supper.

PRIEST AND PEOPLE: **Lord, I am not worthy to receive you, but only say the word and I shall be healed.**

We joyfully go to receive Holy Communion. (To receive Communion, we need to have fasted for one hour. This means that we have not eaten or drunk anything except water one hour before Communion.)

When I approach the priest or eucharistic minister, I bow my head to show that I believe Jesus is really present in the Holy Eucharist. The priest or eucharistic minister offers me a Host and says, "The body of Christ."

I answer: **"Amen."** *I receive the Host either on my tongue or in my hand.*

At some Masses I may also receive the blood of Christ under the appearance of wine. The priest or eucharistic minister hands me the chalice and says, "The blood of Christ."

The Body of Christ

*I answer: "**Amen.**" I take a sip from the chalice.*

After receiving Jesus in Holy Communion, I talk to him in my heart. (Sometimes we might also sing another song together to thank Jesus for coming to us.) I can tell Jesus how much I love him. I can ask for his help for myself and for other people.

Stand

After everyone has received Communion, the priest says a prayer that changes every Sunday.

PEOPLE: **Amen.**

CONCLUDING RITE

We get ready to go home now. Our hearts are filled with the love of Jesus. We are happy to go and bring that love to everyone we meet.

PRIEST: The Lord be with you.

PEOPLE: **And also with you.**

PRIEST: May almighty God bless you, the Father, and the Son, ✠ and the Holy Spirit.

We make the Sign of the Cross and answer: **Amen.**

PRIEST OR DEACON: Go in peace to love and serve the Lord.

PEOPLE: **Thanks be to God.**